A MISSING HEAD EDITION
Ulvåsa 102, 591 95 Motala, Sweden
amissinghead@gmail.com

Printed in the United States of America
ISBN 978-91-519-8204-5

A Quick Look Back

1946
Roswell 1947
1948
1949
1950
1951
Isola di Capri 1952
1953
ROCK AROUND THE CLOCK 1954
1955
Coca Cola
1956
1957
1958
1959
1960
1961
1962!
1963
1964
1966
1968

ANDERS NEUMULLER

A Quick Look Back
1945-2020

To Hamida

Not to speak of Abdul, Adam, Agneta, Aira, Alain, Alec, Alexander, Alice, Alona, Aliya, Amin, Anar, Anders, Andrea, Andreas, Anita, Angela, Angelo, Anke, Ann, Ann-Charlotte, Ann-Christin, Anna, Annika, Anthony, Antonio, Arafat, Arianne, Arvid, Arzoo, Astrid, Agostino, Aviva, Axel, Barbara, Barbro, Bengt, Berit, Bernard, Bernt, Bertil, Bill, Birgit, Birgitta, Björn, Björn-Christian, Bo, Bob, Bo-Christer, Bobby, Boel, Britt, Buster, Calle, Carina, Carl, Carla, Carl-Gustaf, Carl-Johan, Carl-Ludvig, Carlos, Carlotta, Carola, Carole, Caroline, Catarina, Catherine, Cecilia, Christer, Christian, Christoffer, Claes, Clara, Conny, Dag, Dagmar, Dana, Dante, Daniel, David, Deborah, Diana, Diane, Dilshad, Disa, Domenica, Don, Dorothy, Douglas, Ebba, Ebbe, Eira, Eleanore, Elias, Elin, Ellinor, Elisabeth, Ella, Ellen, Elsa, Elsen, Emy, Enrico, Enzo, Erik, Eva, Eugenio, Farah, Fidde, Frank, Fred, Fredrik, Fredrika, Fredrik-Magnus, Freddy, Gabriella, Georg, George, Gerd, Giorgio, Giovanna, Gitta, Gulzar, Gustaf, Gun, Gun-Britt, Gunilla, Gunnar, Gunnel, Gustav, Göran, Görel, Gösta, Hanna, Hanif, Hans, Hans-Börje, Harald, Harri, Harriet, Hartmund, Helena, Helgard, Helle, Henrik, Henry, Hermine, Hibbe, Hildegard, Hubert, Hugo, Håkan, Ian, Ica, Inez, Inga-Lill, Ingeborg, Ingemar, Inger, Ingrid, Ingvar, Irene, Irina, Jacques, James, Jan, Janet, Janne, Jan-Wilhelm, Jenny, Jens, Jerry, Joan, Johan, John, Jonas, Jorge, Josef, Julia, Julian, Jöns, Jörgen, Kaspar, Karim, Karin, Karl, Katarina, Khatoon, Kay, Kazuko, Kjell, Kerstin, Klas, Klas-Fredrik, Kristin, Kristina, Kristoffer, Kulu, Kurt, Laila, Lance, Lars, Lars Aage, Lawrence, Leif, Lena, Lennart, Leonie, Leonor, Leslie, Lilian, Lily, Lisa, Liss Carin, Lloyd, Lollo, Lorenzo, Loretta, Lottie, Louis, Louise, Love, Lucette, Luisa, Lukas, Lull, Lynne, Mabi, Madeleine, Mahmoud, Magnus, Maj, Manne, Manuel, Maria, Marianne, Marike, Margareta, Marius, Mark, Mats, Maureen, Mauritz, Melanie, Michele, Mikael, Mina, Mira, Mobina, Moe, Mona, Monica, Morgan, Mossadique, Myra, Märta, Nancy, Nathalie, Nazim, Nazma, Nels, Nicola, Nzeera, Odd, Otto, Olivia, Olle, Olof, Orvar, Osa, Ottavia, Pa, Pantaleo, Parviz, Pasquale, Paulette, Paulo, Pax, Peder, Penny, Peppino, Per, Per-Olov, Peter, Petrino, Pia, Pippa, Phil, Pål, Ragnar, Ralph, Raoul, Ramzan, Regina, Renee, Richard, Rickard, Robert, Roger, Roland, Rolf, Rona, Rudolf, Salim, Samir, Sana, Sandra, Sebastian, Shalini, Shehnaz, Sherbanu, Sevilla, Siri, Siv, Sofia, Solveig, Sonja, Stein, Stellan, Sten, Stig, Subach, Sumit, Susanne, Svea, Sven, Teppo, Terence, Theresa, Thomas, Thorsten, Tim, Tonino, Tord, Torsten, Ulf, Ulla, Ulla-Britta, Ulrik, Ulrika, Urban, Usha, Yvonne, Valeria, Vali, Vanja, Veronique, Victoria, Vicki, Vinit, Vittorio, Wendy, Wilhelm, Willy, Winki, Winston, Yasmine, Ylva, Yuri, Zera, Åke, Årad, Åsa (and surely many others that I have missed) who now or once upon a time meant something in this strange collage that is my life.

PROLOGUE

Welcome Dear Reader to a little reflection over times past. Many years have past since I started creating these collages with a little text to remind me of all that I felt was of importance during the year.

I was originally planning to put the designs on plates *a la Fornasetti* to celebrate my 75th birthday, but then came Covid-19 and true to the French poet Stéphane Mallarmés' contention that "everything in the world exists to end up as a book" that is where my collages ended up.

My hope is that the short texts will lead you to a lot of googling and that the pictures will take you back in time! And if you have an old-fashioned analogue book there is space to add what each particular year meant to you personally. Or what the person you are going to give the book to was doing during that year,
for example being born, getting married or just living.

1945

*As the world is finally at peace after World War II, the author is
conceived in the Stockholm archipelago on Midsummer's Eve
as mankind dreams of unlimited happiness and prosperity
in the years to come.*

1946

The author is born as the Bikini A-bomb explodes and Stalin shows his true colours. The Western World embraces new delicacies like bananas, and revolutionary inventions like the ballpoint pen.

1947

SAAB presents its first car while the Roswell UFO steals the show from the first Kashmir war, McCarthyism, the establishment of IMF, Kon-Tiki, the Dead Sea Scrolls, the first "computer" and Dior's New Look.

1948

Folke Bernadotte who negotiated peace between Palestine and Israel and Mahatma Gandhi who peacefully led India to independence, are both assassinated - while the world goes wild over American painter Jackson Pollock.

1949

Music lovers welcome the RCA 45 rpm vinyl disc, but the big news otherwise is George Orwell's 1984, the proclamation of the People's Republic of China with Mao Zedong at the helm, and Albert Einstein's formula E=mc2.

1950

The Fifties roll in with the Korean War, the Cold War, Apartheid and the first credit card, but the year will be remembered largely for Disney's Cinderella, the American comic strip Beetle Bailey, James Dean and the scandal of Ingrid Bergman's out-of-wedlock baby.

1951

1951

Mankind receives the Niemeyer/Le Corbusier-designed UN complex in New York and the Suez Canal conflict begins. Dalai Lama surrenders his army and de Gaulle becomes President of France. The start of LEGO.

1952

Queen Elizabeth II succeeds her father, Oslo and Helsinki host the Olympics while further south Capri becomes the playground for King Farouk, Onassis, Grace Fields, Esther Williams, Leni Riefenstahl, Graham Greene, Staffan de Mistura and the author.

1953

Hillary and Tenzing reach the summit of Everest as Queen Elizabeth is crowned and Tetra Pak launches its first packaging for liquids. The first issue of Playboy. The Korean War ends, CIA supports the Shah of Iran as the democratically elected president is deposed.

1954

Bill Haley's Rock Around the Clock marks the start of the rock music revolution. The Algerian War. Eisenhower warns of communism in Vietnam. There is a solar eclipse in Sweden, polio vaccin trials show promise and Hemingway gets the Nobel Prize in Literature.

1955

Consumers welcome Disneyland, tv-dinners, McDonalds and Coke cans. The Guinness Book of Records. Rosa Parks is arrested for not giving up her seat to a white man, while Khrushchev forms the Warsaw Pact and Eisenhower launches the Nautilus nuclear sub.

1956

Russia crushes the Hungarian uprising, Nasser nationalizes the Suez Canal and Brazil gets a new capital. The year of the first Eurovision Song Contest, hard drive, Tefal non-stick, the Sony transistor radio, and Elvis Presley.

1957

The Soviet Union wins the space race with the Sputnik 1 satellite, the Treaty of Rome establishes what was to become the European Union while the world goes gaga over Brigitte Bardot, and news of a contraceptive pill.

1958

The Great Chinese Famine kills more than 30 million while world population reaches the 3 billion mark, Sweden gets its first female priests and Volvo as a first installs three-point safety belts in all its vehicles.

1959

A Russian satellite brings the first image of the far side of the moon, the Cuban revolution makes heroes of Che and Castro. Dalai Lama is exiled, the start of the Vietnam War. First AIDS case recorded in Kinshasa. Hawaii and Alaska become states.

1960

Sugar and television consumption shoot up the year that brings the pill, the laser, the Xerox copier and the Twist. The first televised presidential debate in US history takes place between Kennedy and Nixon. A U-2 spy plane is shot down by the Soviet Air Defence Forces. Muhammed Ali wins a gold medal at the Rome Olympics, and there are seventeen new independent states in Africa.

1961

The first man in space and the first Ken doll. The Berlin Wall goes up. The UN Secretary General Dag Hammarskjold is killed. President Eisenhower warns of the Military Industrial Complex in his farewell address to the nation.

1962

*The Cuban Missile Crisis leads to a Hot Line being set up between
Washington and Moscow, Rachel Carson's Silent Spring brings
environmental concerns to the American public and with it numerous
changes, Breakthroughs for Pop Art, Yves Saint Laurent and
the Rolling Stones. Marilyn Monroe takes an overdose.*

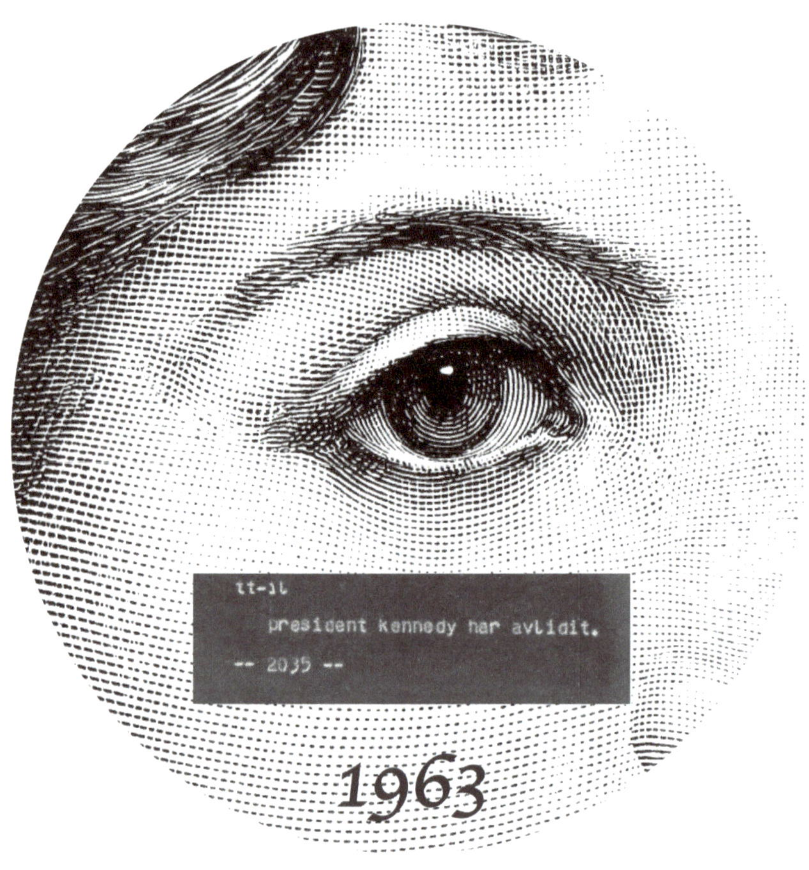

1963

The assassination of President John F Kennedy shocks the world.
The first Beatles record, the first James Bond movie and
the Great Train Robbery. Kenya gains independence,
Iceland gains a volcanic island.

1964

Jean Paul Sartre declines the Nobel Prize in Literature, as China gets its A-bomb and America gets Jeopardy! and the Ford Mustang. Stockholm hosts the first big Pop Art exhibition making stars of Warhol and Lichtenstein.

1965

Doctor Zhivago and The Sound of Music hit the screens.
Skateboarding goes mainstream. Canada gets its maple leaf.
The Mont Blanc tunnel opens and the St. Louis Gateway Arch is
inaugurated. Malcom X is shot. The Watts riots in Los Angeles
highlight racial segregation while racial discrimination in voting
is prohibited by the Voting Rights Act.

1966

Walt Disney dies, Mao publishes his little red book,
a B52 inadvertently drops four hydrogen bombs over Spain, and
London becomes "Swinging London" with Twiggy, the Beatles and
a Labour government.

1967

*Israel attacks its Arab neighbours in the Six Day War and
Indira Gandhi becomes Prime Minister of India, while young people
around the world embrace Flower Power and Hair.
Sweden switches to right hand traffic and the movie Are you curious -
Yellow shakes things up.*

1968

*Protests and social unrest in Paris, Prague, Mexico City,
Washington DC and even Stockholm. The My Lai massacre
becomes a turning point in the Vietnam War. Black Power salutes
at the Olympics. The assassinations of Robert Kennedy and Martin
Luther King. The artist meets the love of his life.*

1969

Apollo moon landing. First flight of Boeing 747. Golda Meir becomes the first female PM of Israel. Rupert Murdoch expands into the United Kingdom. Sweden bans DDT, embraces pizza and elects Olof Palme. Richard Nixon takes power. Woodstock attracts an audience of more than 400 000 as Make Love Not War becomes the new mantra. First HIV death in the US.

1970

Bar code. Aswan High Dam completed after 11 years of construction.
Biafra surrenders, Beatles break up. Cambodia invasion. A cyclon
in Bangladesh kills 500 000. Four students are shot at Kent State.

1971

IRA. Idi Amin. The voting age is lowered to 18 years in UK and USA and Swiss women get the right to vote. The microprocessor, floppy disc, Etch-a-Sketch. The movie French Connection set to be a classic. Commonwealth citizens lose the right to automatic permanent residence in the UK.

1972

The Munich massacre. Nixon visits China and USSR. Watergate.
Olof Palme demonstrates against the Vietnam War. MASH,
Bobby Fischer, Björn Borg and Fritz the Cat rule. The digital watch.
UN conference on the Environment held in Stockholm.

1973

Surgeon Barbie. KISS. Henry Kissinger's New World Order.
Pinochet seizes power in Chile. Yom Kippur War and the first oil crisis.
The Bosphorus Bridge in Istanbul and the Sydney Opera House
inaugurated. A new king in Sweden. A bank robbery with hostages
christens the phenomenon Stockholm Syndrome.

1974

World population reaches 4 billion. Richard Nixon resigns.
"Lucy" australopithecus skeleton found in Ethiopia.
Patty Hearst is kidnapped. ABBA. Rubik's cube.
Pizzas gain popularity in Sweden.

1975

JAWS. End of Vietnam War. US-Soviet space link-up.
The history of contemporary Spain begins following the death of Franco.
Margaret Thatcher becomes conservative party leader.
North Sea oil begins to flow.

1976

*Mao dies. Ebola in Sudan, earthquakes in Italy and China and a
tidal wave in the Phillipines. Jimmy Carter elected President of the US.
Pol Pot becomes prime minister of Cambodia. USA Bicentennial.
Soweto uprising. Björn Borg wins his first Wimbledon title.
Everybody is reading Roots. Apple Computer 1 released.
CN Tower in Toronto completed. Hotel California by the Eagles.
Sex Pistols infamous UK tour.*

1977

Disco Queen Grace Jones and Arnold Schwartzenegger star in Conan while Star Wars is a blockbuster hit. Elvis and Steven Biko die. Wine overtakes spirits in sales in Sweden.

1978

A unique year with three Popes, one possibly murdered.
VW stops production of the Beetle, Saturday Night Fever rules and
in Jonestown they drank the Kool-Aid.
The first daughter of the author is born.

1979

The second oil crisis. Khomeini returns to Iran and the Shah flees. Wars in Afghanistan, Vietnam, Cambodia, Uganda and El Salvador. Three Mile Island nuclear accident. Nobel Peace Prize to Mother Teresa.

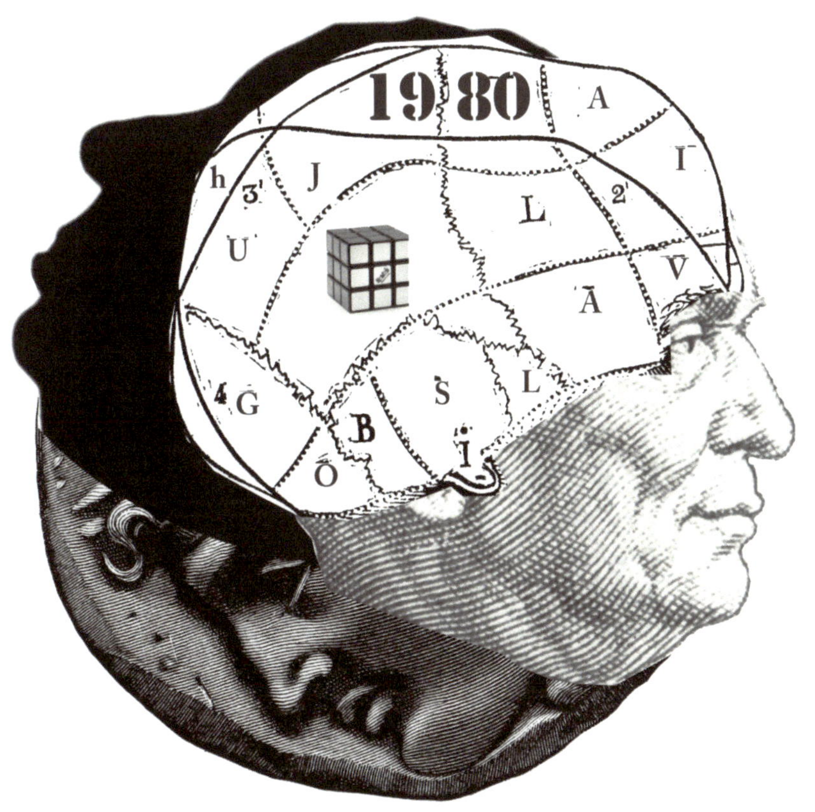

1980

Maze arcade game Pac-man released. Mount St. Helen eruption. Iran-Iraq war. Global eradication of smallpox. Hitchcock and John Lennon die. CNN makes its debut. Terry Fox ends Marathon of Hope. Ronald Reagan, Vigdis Finnbogadottir, Pierre Trudeau win elections. The creator of modern Yugoslavia Tito is honoured with the largest state funeral in history.

1981

Attempted assassination of the Pope and Reagan. Anwar Sadat
assassinated at a military parade. 52 US hostages released in Iran.
The Solidarity union in Poland gains popularity. Post-it Notes.
A Soviet sub runs aground in Sweden. The Medjurgorje apparition.
MTV and the video game Donkey Kong launched. AIDS.
Prince Charles weds Diana Spencer. And so much more this year.
The birth of the author's second daughter.

1982

Recession in USA. First computer virus. Final ABBA performance.
First CD player. Falklands War. Israel invades Lebanon. Ebony And
Ivory, the number one single by Stevie Wonder and Paul McCartney.
The Canada Act ends Britain's power over the country's constitution.
Princess Grace of Monaco dies. E.T.

1983

Mario Brothers, Cabbage Patch kids, Hooters restaurants.
The yacht Australia II wins America's Cup. US invades Grenada.
4 million die in Ethiopian famine. First Costco store opens in Seattle.
President Reagan's Star Wars initiative. Swatch. GPS.

1984

The Golden Temple in Amritsar is occupied and Indira Gandhi is assassinated. Union Carbide responsible for Bhopal gas tragedy. Bob Geldorf's Band Aid for Africa. Desmond Tutu Nobel Peace Laureate. Lichtenstein grants women the right to vote.

1985

Gorbatjov ends the Cold War. Rock Hudson succumbs to aids.
Windows 1.0. Titanic wreck located. Boris Becker, 17, wins Wimbledon.
The movie Out of Africa wins multiple awards. New Coke fails.
We are the world and Live Aid concert raises 125 million dollars to
feed starving Ethiopians.

1986

Chernobyl. Irangate. Swedish PM Olof Palme assassinated.
Mad Cow. Hailey's Comet. Marcos and Baby Doc flee. Ex Nazi,
ex UN Secretary General Kurt Waldheim elected President of Austria.
In Bangladesh hailstones weighing up to one kilo kill 92.

1987

*World population hits the 5 billion mark. Another landslide for
Margaret Thatcher. "Tear down this wall", says Reagan. Supernova.
American televangelist Jim Bakker brought down by scandals.
"Greed is good". Stock market crash. Prozac. Simpsons.
A German teenager lands his Cessna airplane on Red Square.
First criminal conviction based on DNA evidence.*

1988

Iran-Iraq war ends leaving behind 1,5 million casualties.
Soviet withdraws from Afghanistan. Pan Am 103 explodes over Lockerbie.
Operation Black Thunder flushes out Sikh militants from Golden Temple.
Expo88 in Brisbane. Seoul & Calgary Olympics. "World's Fastest Man"
Ben Johnson disqualified. Roxette. Rain Man is the highest grossing film.

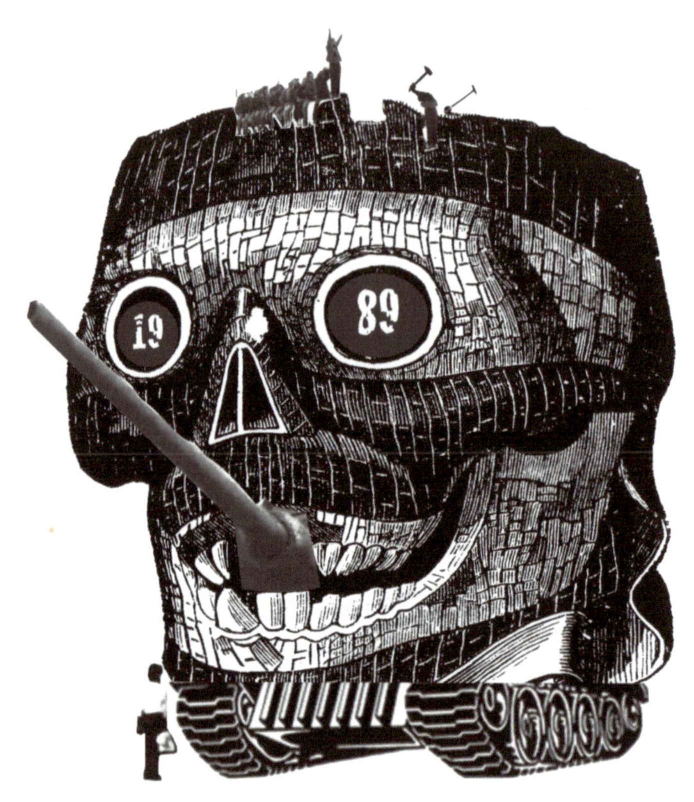

1989

Thousands of democracy protestors killed in Beijing's Tiananmen Square. The fall of the Berlin Wall. Exxon Valdez oil spill. The fatwa against Salman Rushdie. Rumanian dictator Ceauşescu holds his final speech before facing execution.

1990

East and West Germany unite.
The US Ambassador gives Iraq the go-ahead to invade Kuwait.
Nelson Mandela released after 27 years in prison. US enters recession.
First web page. Hubble Space Telescope. Twin Peaks.

1991

*Riot grrrl, Anita Hill confronts US Supreme Court nominee
Clarence Thomas, Third-wave feminism. Thelma and Louise.
South Africa repeals apartheid laws. Freddie Mercury dies.
The Soviet Union breaks up giving independence to Ukraine,
Belarus, Latvia, Estonia, Lithuania, Uzbekistan, Tajikistan,
Kyrgyzstan, Azerbaijan and Moldova.*

1992

Earth Summit in Rio. In Sweden the interest rate rises to 500%.
Rodney King and LA riots. Two big earthquakes rock California.
CDs beat cassette tapes. The dissolution of the Socialist Federal
Republic of Yugoslavia, Sarajevo besieged by Serbian troops.

1993

Oslo Accord, Maastricht Treaty, NAFTA Agreement. Waco Siege.
Eritrea splits from Ethiopia. Russian troops leave Poland and Lithuania.
Blackhawk Down, the Battle of Mogadishu.
Storm of the Century in North America. Jurassic Park.
Jack in the Box E. coli outbreak

1994

Half a million killed in Rwanda massacre.
852 die when MS Estonia sinks in the Baltic Sea.
The world's first mass commercial internet spam campaign.
Nuclear weapons de-targeting agreement between USA, Russia and
China. Channel Tunnel opens. O.J Simpson acquitted.
Lion King, Friends. Genetically engineered tomatoes.

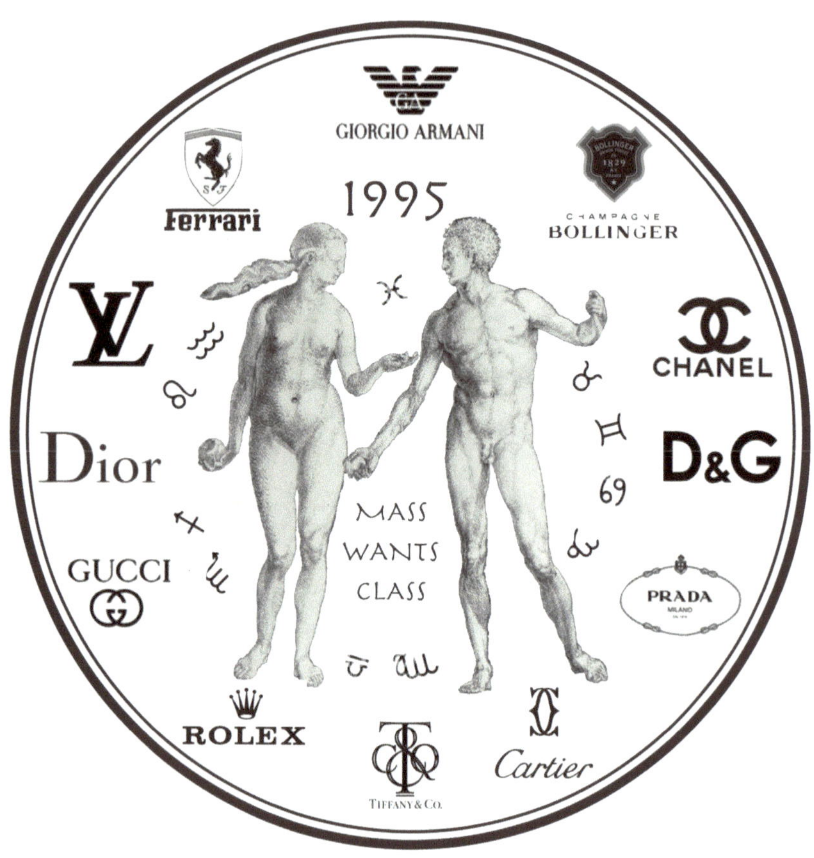

1995

Sweden, Denmark and Finland join the EU. US bails out Mexico. Sarin gas attack in Tokyo metro. Oklahoma City bombing. Screbernica massacre. Rabin (and Palestine peace deal) killed. Launch of Windows95. Seinfeld, Goldeneye, Batman, Toy Story.

1996

The Centennial of the Olympics marked with the introduction of golf,
softball, mountain biking and beach volleyball in Atlanta.
Mad Cow Disease. Dolly the cloned sheep. Charles and Di divorce.
Pokemon, DVDs and La Macarena are all the rage.
Launch of Fox News and Ebay.

1997

1997

IBM computer beats chess champion Kasparov. Bird flu. El Nino.
Death of Princess Diana, Versace and Mother Teresa.
Septuplets born in Iowa. Heaven's Gate sect suicide.
First Harry Potter book. Tiger Woods wins the Masters Tournament.
The movie Titanic receives multiple awards.

1998

Google. Viagra. Clinton-Lewinsky scandal.
India conducts three, and Pakistan five nuclear tests respectively.
Terrorists bomb US embassies in Kenya and Tanzania.
Sweden criminalizes the purchase of sex.
Hugo Chavez president of Venezuela.

1999

*The world pays $448 billon to counter the threat of the Y2K bug.
NATO bombs Belgrade. Columbine and Finland school shootings.
Mandela steps down. Putin succeeds Yeltsin as President of Russia.
Total solar eclipse. Euro. Super cyclone kills 10 000 in India.*

2000

*The International Year of Peace. Indian population hits 1 billion.
Big mergers. Bridge between Sweden and Denmark opens to traffic.
Concorde crash. Snoopy's father Charles M. Schulz dies.*

2001

The September 11 attacks and the War on Terrorism in Afghanistan.
Wikipedia launched. The Pentagon cannot account for $2,3 trillion.
The first space tourist, the iPod is launched and earthquakes
in Gujarat, Peru and El Salvador.

2002

SARS. Guantanamo Bay Detention Centre.
Israel begins construction of West Bank fence. Bali bombings,
Gujarat riots, Moscow theatre and Bethlehem Nativity Church sieges.
An International Criminal Court established.
Nobel Peace Prize to Jimmy Carter.

2003

USA and UK attack Iraq on false pretext of Weapons of Mass Destruction. Czech Republic, Estonia, Poland, Latvia, Malta, Slovenia, Slovakia join EU. 99% human DNA mapped. Blackouts. London congestion tax.

2004

Indian Ocean earthquake and tsunami kills 200 000. Mars landings.
Orange revolution in Ukraine. World of Warcraft wows online players.
RMS Queen Mary 2 sets sail. Dan Rather, Martha Stewart,
Janet Jackson and Justin Timberlake scandals.
Farenheit 451 receives a Retro Hugo Award.

2005

Pope John Paul II dies. Angela Merkel Chancellor of Germany.
YouTube. IRA lays down its arms. Airbus 380, the largest passenger
plane in the world, makes its maiden flight. Hurricane Katrina.
North American ice storm. Earthquakes in Kashmir, Iran, Sumatra.
China-Russia military exercise. Prince Charles marries Camilla.

2006

2006

Ceasefires in Burundi, Congo, Uganda, Sudan and Spain.
Nigeria and Camerun and India and Pakistan make peace.
Iraq is in a mess. Israel invades Lebanon.
Nobel Peace Prize goes to Muhammad Yunus.
An Inconvenient Truth. Spotify founded.

2007

iPhone mania. Al Gore receives Nobel Peace Prize.
Worthless subprime mortgages. US obesity epidemic.
Virginia Tech shooting. Drug-resistant TB.
Angola's BNP up 24% (China 12%).
Benazir Bhutto assassinated. Ingmar Bergman dies.

2008

Global financial crisis. Russia-Georgia war. Israel invades Gaza.
Terrorist attack in Bombay. Food and fuel unrest in Third World.
Beijing Olympics. Bitcoin. Spotify launched.
Barak Obama elected president. Putin and Medvedev switch jobs.
Bionic eyes give hope to the blind.

2009

H1N1, Swine flu pandemic, Bernie Madoff's ponzi scheme and the end of the US recession. Iceland economy collapses and Greenland achieves self-government. The movie Slumdog Millionaire is a hit. President Barak Obama receives the Nobel Peace Prize.

2010

WikiLeaks and Julian Assange. Haiti earthquake.
Iceland volcano stops air traffic.Vuvuzelas make FIFA news.
Burj Khalifa inaugurated in Dubai. iPad and Instagram are launched.
3D computer-animated film Despicable Me.
Iraq war has cost the US $3 trillion so far.
Interbreeding between Neanderthals and humans confirmed.

2011

Arab Spring and start of Syrian War. Utøya massacre.
Osama Bin Laden is killed. Third expansion of World of Warcraft.
Kim Jong Il dies. 9,9 earthquake and tsunami devastates Japan.
Occupy Wall Street. William marries Kate.
Global population hits 7 billion.

2012

Costa Concordia sinking. Group rape in Delhi shocks the world.
Turanor first solar electric vehicle to circumnavigate the globe.
Facebook buys Instagram. Encyclopedia Britannica goes digital.
Sandy Hook school shooting. Life of Pi is filmatized.
EU bans incandescent light bulbs and gets the Nobel Peace Prize.

2013

China moon landing, huge meteor in Russia and Indian mission to Mars. 3D-printed ear. 2 500 protesters killed in Egypt. Demonstrations in Hongkong in support of Edward Snowden. 12 years a slave. The Pope resigns. The author moves back to Sweden.

2014

ISIS, Ebola, school shootings and legalization of marijuana. Russia annexes Crimea. The movie Interview featuring Kim Jong Vu makes waves, Conchita Wurst wins the Eurovision Song Contest and Malala gets the Nobel Peace Prize.

2015

*1,6 million refugees make their way to the EU. 60 million people
displaced world-wide. Greek debt crisis. Water found on Mars.
Charlie Hebdo magazine attacked in Paris by Al-Qaeda.
The Volkswagen emissions scandal. Mad Max: Fury Road.*

2016

Prince, David Bowie and the poet Leonard Cohen (who should have received the Nobel Prize in Literature instead of singer-song-writer Bob Dylan) die in the midst of Brexit and Trump woes.

2017

MeToo dominates the news while sun power edges out oil and 32-year old Crown Prince Muhammad bin Salman ("MBS") tightens his grip on power in Saudi Arabia, buying Leonardo da Vincis's Salvator Mundi in the process.

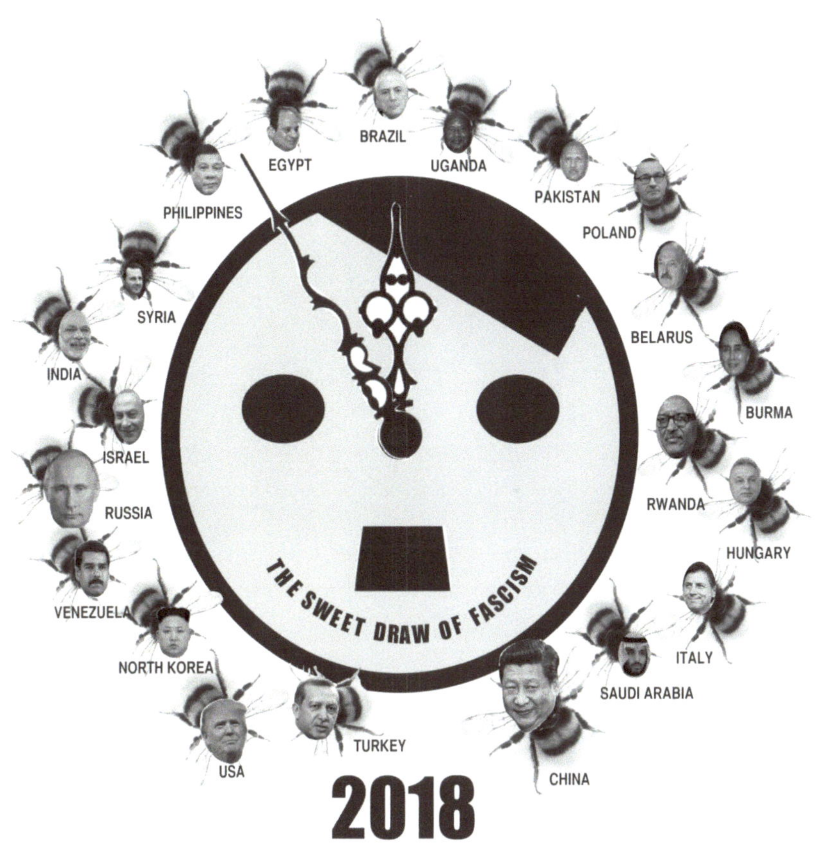

2018

Xi Jinping becomes leader for life as Trump starts a trade war with China. A journalist is murdered in the Saudi consulate in Istanbul. More plastic than fish in the sea. Scientists propose a ten year deadline to halt global warming. Streaming beats CDs and vinyl.

2019

Afghanistan, Sri Lanka, Congo, Bogota attacks. Trump. Brexit.
Hong Kong protests. IS defeated? Hottest October ever.
Greta Thunberg gives a face to global warming concerns.
New Japanese Emperor, Thai King and Brazilian President.

2020

Mostly COVID-19, but also AI, the opioid and grasshopper invasions, the Hong Kong and George Floyd riots, Bezos' Amazon, the Beirut explosion,Judge Ruth Gaber Ginsburg's death, and Trump's pranks and electoral defeat

A Quick History of the Collage

1

The conventional truth is that collage arrived on the art scene in Paris in 1912, but I believe we should go back further in time.

Paper was invented in China around 200 BC. The new material and the many ways it was cut, combined, decorated, and written and painted on, must have produced many (easily destroyed) art works through the ages.

We do know that in the 10th century Japanese calligraphers used different kinds of paper and glue in a collage fashion to enhance poetry texts. In the early 18th century cut-out portrait silhouettes and scenes became popular as did "paper-mosaics". There are also Victorian albums with cut-out photographs of people glued on to water colour painted backgrounds in a collage fashion.

"Paper cutting is the prelude to writing," wrote **Hans Christian Andersen** (1805-1875). The Danish fairy tale author was as good with his scissors as he was with his pen. He demonstrated his skill at parties, usually folding a piece of paper in the middle and then cutting around the axis, producing a symmetrical picture when the paper was unfolded. His very modern-looking fantasy paper cut-outs of (1) a "sunflower person", palaces and small scenes or birds, houses or his characters, are now recognized as art. But when they were made and usually casually given away, the cut-outs had no perceived value which has generally been the way that collage as art has been treated.

The art world takes style seriously and collage was regarded as an offshoot or by-product of the development of Cubism. So even though collage has been used by artists in movements such as Dada, Modernism, Surrealism, Futurism, Russian Constructivism, Abstract Expressionism, Anti-art, Pop Art, etcetera, it has not generally been accepted as a style in its own right. When, for example, paper bits were added to a painting for a three-dimensional "sculptural effect" the juxtaposition simply became an "at once serious and tongue-in-cheek" *addition.*

The beginnings

For seven years George Braque and Pablo Picasso met almost every day as they developed Cubism. Their paintings from this period are often so interchangeable that it is difficult to identify the artist.

Experts believe that **Braque** was first to use the collage technique. This was in 1912 when he bought a roll of simulated oak-grain paper, the kind used for shelves and drawers. Cut out pieces of this paper were attached to Braque's charcoal drawing of a guitar to simulate a wood surface.

Pablo Picasso, who was known to be a keen observer of any new development among his colleagues, quickly realized the significance of this breakthrough and he subsequently became the first artist to employ the *papiers collés* technique on oil paintings. He also bought "oil cloth" paper but with a caning pattern for his 1912 oval (2) *Still Life with Chair Caning* that is framed with a rope. In the painting you see a knife, glass, napkin, a lemon and the words JOU for "game" or more likely "journal" as the picture has a lot of what you would expect to see when visiting a French café.

The DADA movement in Europe and North America blamed the military, royalty, nationalism, colonialism and the bourgeois capitalist society for all ills. In this process they also rejected traditional aesthetics. The German artist (with the anglicized name) **John Heartfield** (1891-1968) went beyond most others in his use of art as a political weapon on posters and in newspapers. His *photomontages* like (3) *Hurrah, There's No Butter Left!* (with a quote by Göring saying ""Iron has always made an empire strong, butter and lard have made a people fat at most.") 1935, depicts a Nazi family feasting on a bike. The Dadaist and committed communist had to flee Berlin and Germany when Hitler came to power, becoming number 5 on the Nazi Most Wanted list.

In his later life when the renowned painter **Henri Matisse** (1869-1954) was bed-ridden, he turned his need for an artistic outlet to *cut-outs*. Using a large pair of scissors, he cut out shapes from boldly coloured paper and had his assistants move them around and then nail them to the wall, eventually transforming the compositions into lithographs. His (4) *Icarus*, appeared as an illustration in the book *Jazz*, falling from the sky surrounded by WW2 mortar fire.

Matisse's friend Picasso, who lived nearby in the south of France, was impressed, but one critic described the old-new art form as "paper jokes". The Tate Gallery in London noted a record-breaking number of visitors when it exhibited Henri Matisse's cut paper collages in 2014.

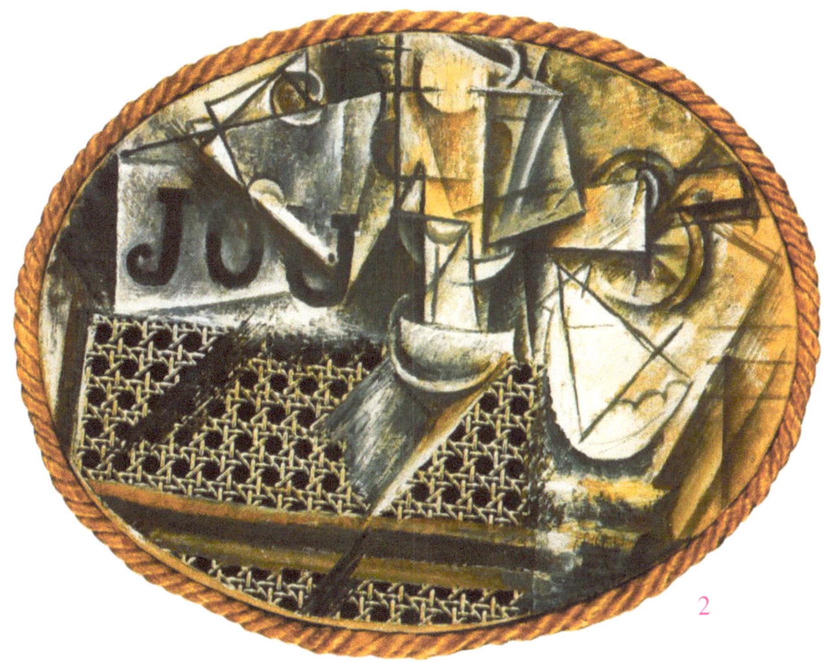

2

3

Hurrah, die Butter ist alle!
Goering in seiner Hamburger Rede: „Erz hat stets ein Reich stark gemacht,
Butter und Schmalz haben höchstens ein Volk fett gemacht".

4

Dada and Surrealism

Many art historians see DADA as the beginning of abstract art, performance art and Surrealism. **Hanna Höch** (1889-1978) used real photographs or printed images to perfect the DADA photomontage in (5) *Für ein Fest gemacht* (Made for a Party) 1936 and other work. The bisexual artist personified Dada's "New Woman, "financial, sexual and free to vote" ideal but was never completely accepted by the rather sexist male Dada artists. She was the only Dadaist to defy the Nazis by remaining in Berlin even though they deemed her work "degenerate". She also wrote the *The Painter* about "an artist who is thrown into an intense spiritual crisis when his wife asks him to do the dishes."

One of the founders of the Cologne DADA group was **Max Ernst** (1891-1976) who became famous as a Surrealist. He left his family in Germany for a *menage a trois*, first in Paris and then in Bangkok, before marrying the art collector Peggy Guggenheim and moving to New York. Ernst developed the *frottage* (pencil rubbings) and *grattage* (fresh paint scratching) techniques, but above all collage. His (6) *Birdman* from the poetic novel *Une semaine de bonté* (A Week of Kindness) 1934, has no words but 182 surreal collages using old engraved illustrations from dictionaries and novels.

The Radnitzky family shortened their surname to Ray when they moved to Queens and their son Emmanuel later shortened his name to Man. **Man Ray** (1890-1976) wanted to become a painter, but after meeting the Dadaist Marcel Duchamp he went off on a tangent. He started making "readymades", sculptures with a collage twist, like the unusable flat iron (7) *The Gift* 1921 that he made the same day as his first exhibit.

After moving to Paris Man Ray became known for fashion shoots and photographs of the leaders of the modern art scene, but above all for transforming photography into art, with innovations like *rayographs* (objects placed on photographic paper and then exposed) and *solarization* (exposing a print or negative to a flash of light during development to give it a sort of halo effect).

Man Ray's colliborator, assistant and lover Lee Miller, is famous in her own right as a model, war photographer (with an iconic photo of herself in Hitler's bath tub) and cook. Another lover was the artist's model Alice Prin, the "Queen of Montparnasse", whom Man Ray photographed for (8) *Le Violon d'Ingres* (Ingres's Violin) 1924. By adding the violin's air holes on Prin's body he transformed a classical nude to one of the foremost surrealist works of art. The title was an in joke among the artists in Paris, as the classical painter Ingres, who passionately loved the female body, also played the violin.

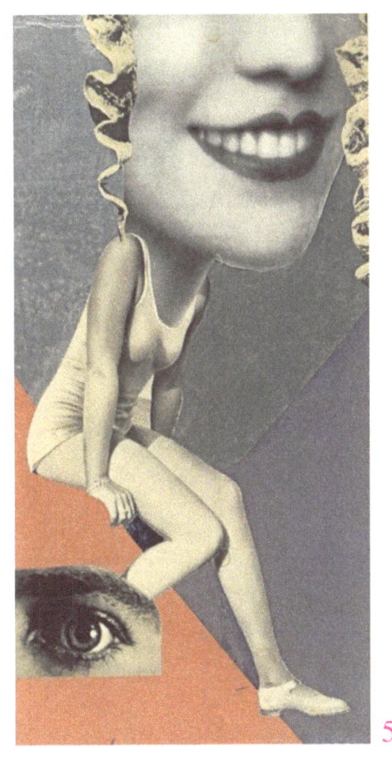

5

6

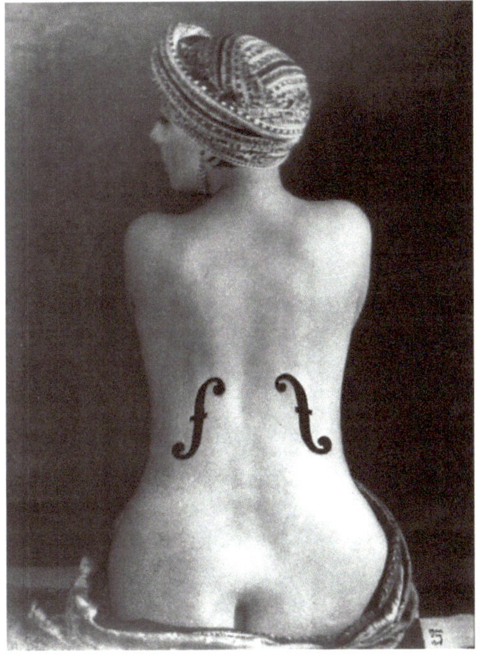

8

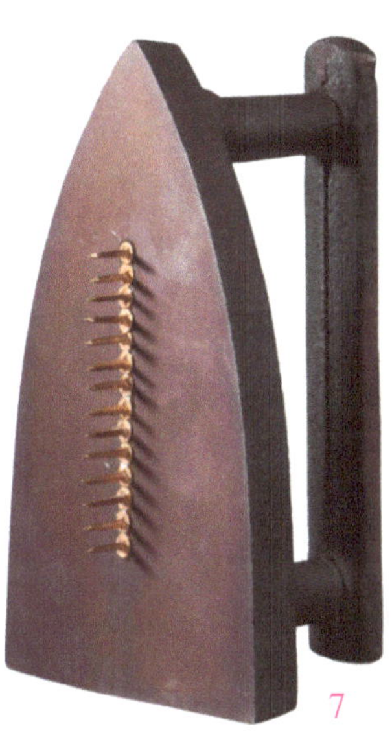

7

Another dimension

In 1930, Louis Aragon organised an exhibition in Paris dedicated solely to collage. It included works by Arp, Braque, Dalí, Duchamp, Ernst, Gris, Man Ray, Magritte,Miró, Picabia, Picasso and Tanguy. The works could all be framed.

This was however not possible with the works of the artist and experimental filmmaker **Joseph Cornell** (1903-1972) who made his collages go from flat to three dimensional. His *assemblage* made by grouping together objects in a wooden box like his (9) *Fortune Telling Parrot* (Parrot Music Box) 1938. Cornell built up a "library" of oddities from secondhand bookstores and flea markets and created works like the *Medici Slot Machine* series and the *Space Objects* in self-made wooden shadow boxes. Among his finds was also a B movie that he spliced together in an entirely new collage fashion. He mostly gave away his work. The recipient of an *Owl Box* was Audrey Hepburn.

Cornell spent all his life on Utopia Parkway in Queens caring for his mother and his ailing brother, but he filled his boxes with dreams of foreign travel and love. A loner, he was still part of the art scene, hanging out with everybody from Dalí and Duchamp to Warhol and Matta. It was a Max Ernst collage novel that made him see "that art was not necessarily a matter of applying paint to canvas, but could also be made from real objects, estrangingly combined."

When we think of Pop Art, it is American artists who come to mind. But it was actually a Brit who pioneered the art form with (10) *Just What Is It That Makes Today's Homes So Different, So Appealing?* 1956. **Richard Hamilton** (1922-2011) filled an ad for a linoleum floor with the Pop staples "Man, Woman, Food, History, Newspapers, Cinema, Domestic Appliances, Cars, Space, Comics, TV, Telephone, Information" blurring the boundaries between "high" art and "low" culture. He made Pop Art fun and upheld the notion that art can borrow from any source. A teacher of art, he regarded his pupil Bryan Ferry, who started Roxy Music, as "his greatest creation."

When you furnish a home you can choose between lots of different styles, but the style that reigns supreme in magazines is always *Eclectic*. This is when you mix old and new and historical styles so that your home becomes a collage of sorts, just like a Mood Board or Instagram feed. Hamilton's US colleague **Tom Wesselmann** (1931-2004) did not like the Pop Art label, but his eclectic (11) *Great American Nude No. 44* 1963 incorporates a radiator, telephone, coat, door and a reproduction of a classical painting. Another of his installations has a turned-on television set, taking collage to a sculptural level that also includes almost all of the senses.

9

10

11

Personal favourites

I want to tell you about three works that hang on my own walls - by very different artists and in different styles of collage.

As a kid growing up in Stockholm, I loved the concrete play sculpture in the Humlegården park. It looked a bit like a dragon and you could climb all over it and slide down or hide in it. This was a creation of the Danish architect and sculptor **Egon Möller-Nielsen** (1915-1959) who was also the illustrator of the very creative children's book *Historien om någon* (The story about someone) in which you follow little clues page by page until you realize that you have been following a little kitten.

Recently I found Möller-Nielsen's collage (12) *Vindflöjel* (Weather Vane) 1941 in a limited artist's magazine. With drawings, cut and even burnt coloured paper, silk paper and a leaf (that I had to re-attach) the happy-looking assembly is quite typical for early collages.

In Vancouver my wife ran the popular gallery/café Teatime where a new artist exhibited every month. The show of the Saskatchewan collage artist **Chuck Crate** (1915-1992) included (13) *An Outline of History* 1982 that we we fell in love with and bought. Like all his work it is meticulously executed and so well varnished it almost looks like a Russian icon. Crate was a teacher, gold miner, union organizer, First Nations rights activist and lexicographer. But everybody has their secrets. When I was trying to obtain a photograph of Crate, I found out, thanks to Wikipedia, that he at age 17 had also been the leader of the Canadian Union of Fascists.

During the Watergate scandal, posters featuring President Nixon were plastered all over Stockholm. It was the Norwegian-Swedish artist **Kjartan Slettemark** (1932-2008) who had combined the official picture of Richard Nixon with the coffee cup and hand from a Gevalia coffee advertisement poster and to that added captions like "Speed kills!", "Friendship and Freedom Forever" and "Ein Reich, Ein Führer". He later cut the posters into small pieces and created collages like the (14) *Nixon Visions*.

For his passport picture he took the face of Nixon and combined it with his own hair and beard. This passport later fetched half a million kronor at an auction.

KjARTan had a dadaist "unintellectual attitude to art", working with all kinds of reused container finds, techniques and video in a Pop Art way. When he was diagnosed as borderline by social services he made a happening out of it. He also staged himself as a naked Marilyn Monroe with a blonde wig and a bright red mouth made out of a lid. And another time for a show and an opening he dressed up as a white King Poodle, even biting an art critic. Kjartan Slettemark was really art himself.

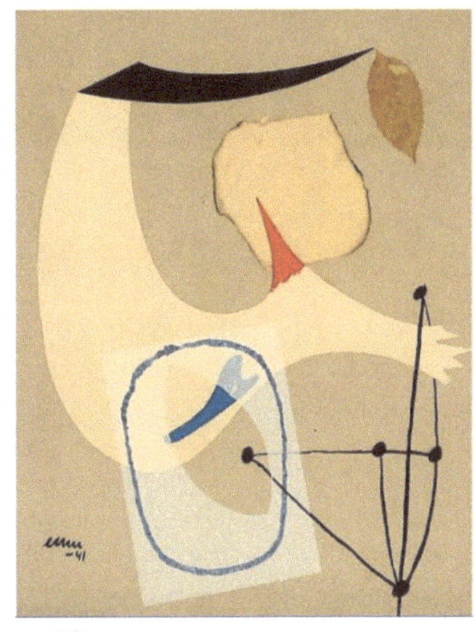

12

13

14

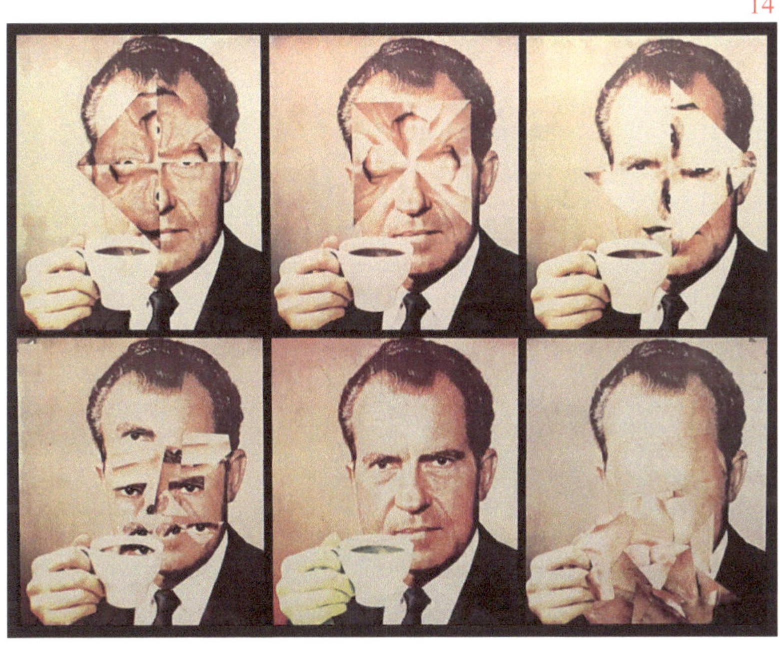

Right now

As all the artists I have written about so far are dead, you may wonder how collage is faring today. Digital media has moved the focus from paper, but many artists still love the quick hands-on use of discarded material transforming the un-extraordinary into something new. Collage is huge on social media thanks to photography and new apps, but it is an art form that can also be found in literature, music, movies, gaming, magazines and in the advertising world.

Collages are still big on issues like MeToo and BlackLivesMatter but politics and topical themes have taken a step back with much more emphasis on the personal and the universal. One reason for this could be copyright laws and the EU GDPR privacy law that can make a legal issue out of a face or even a body part used in a work of art. This explains why you will not find a single face in the collage posters and art offered at, for example, IKEA.

Daily Mail Style Editor **Emily Monckton**'s (born 1995) poodle (15) *Frida* and other pooches appear in her colourful collages with lots of fashion, bling and use of vintage magazines.

Greek-born **Eugenia Loli** (born 1973) is one of the most productive artists in the US with absurdities like (16) *Rising Mountain*.

In the movie *The Secret Life of* **Lance Letcher** (b.1962) we learn about the artist's dysfunctional childhood and his insights on creativity, the subconscious and spirituality. In his large (17) *Hand* he uses coloured Nigerian metal scraps instead of paper.

Kenyan-born **Wangechi Mutu** (born 1972) uses all kinds of unexpected materials in her collage works, including tea, feathers and sand, as she wrangles with colonial pre-conceptions. Mutu's fantastical collage figures are also the inspiration for (18) *Ayo Janeen Jackson AKA Miss Appropriation* who has performed at Mutu art auction events.

"I think everything in life is art," says actress Helena Bonham Carter, who I never imagined quoting. "What you do. How you dress. The way you love someone, and how you talk. Your smile and your personality. What you believe in, and all your dreams. The way you drink your tea. How you decorate your home. Or party. Your grocery list. The food you make. How your writing looks. And the way you feel. Life is art." I would like to take this a step further and substitute the word art with *collage*.

Right from its start collage has released the subconscious in a most playful way transcending the ordinary into exceptional works of art. It is still the most accesible, inexpensive and democratic art form around.

So if you have tried painting or sculpture without getting the feeling of complete acceptance and fulfillment, you too should have a go at collage.

15

16

17

18

Details and Sites

(1) Art: Hans Christian Andersen, *"sunflower person" fantasy paper cut out, 1845 (reversed), courtesy Odense Bys Museer. Portrait: H C Andersen in 1892, photo by Thora Hallager (detail), courtesy Wikimedia Commons. Site: hcandersensodense.dk (1.5) Portrait: George Braque, courtesy Wikimedia Commons. (2) Art:* Pablo Picasso, *Still Life with Chair Caning, 1912, oil on oil-cloth over canvas edged with rope, 29 x 37 cm, courtesy Musée Picasso. Portrait: Picasso in 1908 (detail), courtesy Wikimedia Commons. Site: pablopicasso.org (3) Art:* John Heartfield *Hurrah, There's No Butter Left!, © 2011-2017 John J Heartfield. Portrait: John Heartfield (detail) courtesy Wikimedia Commons. Site: johnheartfield.com (4) Art:* Henri Matisse *Icarus stencil and litho, plate VIII from the illustrated book "Jazz", 1947. Portrait: Henri Matisse in 1920 (detail), courtesy Wikimedia Commons. Site: henrimatisse.org (5) Art:* Hannah Höch, *Für ein Fest gemacht (Made for a Party) 1936, courtesy Whitechapel Gallery. Portrait: A self portrait (detail) by Hannah Höch, c.1926, courtesy Wikimedia Commons. Sites: moma.org, artnet.com, artsy.net, (6) Art:*Max Ernst *"Birdman" from vol. 3 of Une Semaine de Bonte (A Week of Kindness), 1933, © ADAGP, Portrait: Max Ernst in 1968 (detail), Dutch National Archives, The Hague, courtesy photocollectie Algemeen Nederlands Persbureau (ANEFO), Site: modernamuseet.se/ stockholm/ en/exhibitions/max-ernst/ (7) Art:* Man Ray *The Gift sculpture and readymade consisting of an iron with fourteen thumb tacks glued to its sole, 1921, © Man Ray Trust ARS-ADAGP, now offered as a multiple of 5,000 for $1,127 each by fineartmultiple.com, (8) Art:* Man Ray *Le Violon d'Ingres (Ingres's Violin) 1924 © Man Ray Trust ARS-ADAGP. Portrait: Man Ray (detail) photo by Carl Van Vechten 1934, courtesy Van Vechten Collection, Site: manraytrust.com (9) Art:* Joseph Cornell *Untitled Fortune Telling Parrot (Parrot Music Box) 1938, gift for Carmen Miranda, courtesy Peggy Guggenheim Museum. Portrait: Joseph Cornell (detail) photographed by Hans Namuth, 1971, courtesy Wikimedia Commons. Site: josephcornell.org (10) Art:* Richard Hamilton *Just What Is It That Makes Today's Homes So Different, So Appealing?1956. Kunsthalle Tübingen, Tübingen. Portrait: Richard Hamilton in 1992 (detail), courtesy Wikimedia Commons Site: tate.org.uk/art/artists/richard-hamilton-1244 (11) Art:* Tom Wesselmann, *Still Life #20 mixed media 1962, Collection Albright-Knox Art Gallery, Buffalo, New York © Estate of Tom Wesselmann/Licensed by VAGA at Artists Rights Society (ARS), NY. Portrait: Tom Wesselman (detail), courtesy Wikimedia Commons. Site: operagallery.com/tom-wesselmann (12) Art:* Egon Möller-Nielsen *Vindflöjel (Weather Vane) in the magazine Création 1942, private collection. Portrait: Egon Möller-Nielsen (detail), courtesy Wikimedia Commons, (13) Art:* Chuck Crate *An Outline of History 1982, private collection. Portrait: Detail from an untitled collage by Chuck Crate in the permanent collection of the Dunlop Art Gallery in Regina, Saskatchevan. Site: http://collection. dunlopartgallery.org/ (14) Art:* Kjertan Slettemark *Nixon Visions collage, private collection. Portrait: Kjertan Slettemark's Self portrait (detail) as Marilyn 2007. Site: kjartan.se (15) Art:* Emily Monckton *Frida. Portrait: Emily Monckton (detail) courtesy artist. Site: thefullmontageco.uk (16) Art:* Eugenia Loli *Rising Mountain (art print available from society6.com). Portrait: Eugenia Loli (detail) from publichouseofart.com. Site: facebook.com/eugenialoli (17) Art:* Lance Letscher, *Hand Metal Collage on Board 52 × 40 in, 2016, courtesy Tayloe Piggot Gallery. Portrait: Lance Letscher, Photo by Todd V. Wolfson, Austin Chronicle, 2017. Site: lanceletscher.com (18) Art:* Wangechi Mutu's *fantastical figures has inspired Ayo Janeen Jackson AKA Miss Appropriation, here at a Mutu event. (Photo: Africa's Out! Facebook page). Portrait: Wangechi Mutu (detail), courtesy WikiArt Site:saatchigallery.com/artist/wangechi_mutu*

EPILOGUE

I really hope that you have enjoyed *A Quick Look Back* and that it may become your notebook when you yourself look back!

As this book was truly "homemade" there must be lots of mistakes, so please email any corrections to me at *amissinghead@gmail.com* so that everything can be correct in later editions.

You have of course understood that I am getting on in age, but I can promise you that I will continue with my quest to portray each coming year as long as I live!

I am not active on social media, but you can contact me at *amissinghead@gmail.com* if you want to hear about upcoming annual collages, editions, originals and books, or if you would like to be notified on the rare occasions that I actually do exhibit.

1995
SYDNEY 2000
1997
19 98
Y2K 1999
200i
2002
20 03
2004
20 05
2019
2006
2007
LEHMAN
20 09
2010
vancouver
2011
2012
2013
20 14
2016
MeToo
2017
2018